Everyday wisdom
for Living with Faith

Everyday Wisdom
for Living with Faith

Inspiration for Christians

DIANA FRANSIS ONORATO, MSG

Good Books

New York, New York

Good Books books may be purchased in bulk at special discounts for sales promotion, corporate gifts, fund-raising, or educational purposes. Special editions can also be created to specifications. For details, contact the Special Sales Department, Good Books, 307 West 36th Street, 11th Floor, New York, NY 10018 or info@skyhorsepublishing.com.

Good Books is an imprint of Skyhorse Publishing, Inc.®, a Delaware corporation.

Visit our website at www.goodbooks.com

10 9 8 7 6 5 4 3 2 1

Library of Congress Cataloging-in-Publication Data is available on file.

Cover design by Peter Donahue

Print ISBN: 978-1-68099-434-6
eBook ISBN: 978-1-68099-435-3

Printed in the United States of America

Dedication

This book is dedicated to my husband, Jake Onorato, and my son, Jack Onorato. It is our greatest hope as new parents to raise a son who is always respectful and loving towards others. I am daily guided by Mother Theresa's quote, "If you want to change the world, go home and love your family." Jack, I hope you change the world.

Introduction

This book was created to encompass words of wisdom about living the good life from ordinary individuals in all walks of life. It is meant to open and enlighten our perspectives regarding the world's abundant philosophies, united into one manuscript. Contributors had the opportunity to share their wisdom, bringing light to original words, ideas, and experiences that would have otherwise remained unknown.

Opening this conversation with the rest of the world is a way of honoring all the abundant ways of life, in answer to the question, "If there were anything you could tell the rest of the world, what would it be?"

The goal for this project was to create something that left a feel-good, life-loving impression on others. With the help of many, we've tried to create that feeling, getting as many people involved as we possibly could to share some incredible words of wisdom.

This is a book was written by everybody, for everyone to enjoy.

Focus your energy on rebuilding the world

"I have a great distaste for people who always find something to complain about, because life is too short. If they took that same energy they use for complaining and finding fault, and instead put it toward something constructive, they could rebuild the world."
—Sandy Kaplan

Don't just pass the butter

"I believe in prayer. I pray every night. My prayers
get longer the more friends I have to pray for.
Like [my friend] who lives in my assisted living
community, she is completely paralyzed on her
right side. Her foot, her arms, even her kidneys are
paralyzed. She has been that way for years. She was
that way when I came here, but she is happy. I eat
at the same table with her. I always wait for her to
come down . . . I always sit with her during lunch
and dinner because I help her. She just has her left
hand, so I wait for her and I sit with her and I tear
the sugar packet and hand it to her. She hands me
the bread and I butter it and hand it back to her and
anything else that I can do. So, I guess she is the best
friend that I have here. I always pray for her . . .
I help her because I love her and it's just one little
thing that makes me happy and it makes her happy."
—Ruth Austill

**Have enough to put a meal on the table.
That is enough.**

"I was born in Emporia, Kansas, in a
room upstairs. In those days, during the
depression, very few people could afford a
hospital room. Some of the best years of my
life were during the depression. Everyone
was poor . . . you didn't really realize the
difference between having something and
not having something. If you had enough to
put a meal on the table, that was enough. You
would never think about having something
that someone else had because that other
person had the same thing you did."
—Royce Woodward

Success in Marriage

"Success in marriage has to be give-and-take, in all situations. Don't be stubborn. Whatever you cannot have today, remember that you might tomorrow. I gave my wife everything. Everything she wanted, she got. I went without, of course, but I wasn't a big spender . . . To me, she had a wonderful life in the time she was married. My children also say the same thing, that I couldn't have done anything more for her. She was here one day, then all of a sudden, she was gone at night. She was gone, just like that. It's not a good thing to die of course, but what I can say is that she did not suffer at all. I did whatever I could while she was alive. I took her to the emergency room and they found nothing wrong, then the following day she was gone. That was a shocker because I did not expect for her to pass that way, or at that particular time because she was very healthy, but it happened . . . I miss her because we used to come into the kitchen, have breakfast, a few cups of coffee, and talk for 2 to 3 hours; you name it, we talked about it. And now I get up and everything is silent. I don't see her. I don't talk to her and I miss her . . . I miss her a lot."

—Frank J. Calvillo

Practice respect

"Help people in any way you can. Especially the older people. Just respect people for what they are even if you don't agree with them. Show them that you have enough intelligence that even though you may not agree with what they are saying, you respect them for who they are. That always shows that you were brought up to respect somebody. If you show respect, you gain a lot more knowledge and people will tell you things they may not have ever told you because you don't have an attitude that you know everything."
—Sandra Landan

Success in Life

"If I can be well-adjusted, hard-working, and a healthy individual, I will feel like I have succeeded so that my children can develop to their fullest potential. I don't know if they have developed to their fullest potential or not but they each went their different ways and they all made great lives for themselves—that's one of the things that I determine as true success."
—Alice Fransis

Health

"If I could offer any words of wisdom, they would be to take care of yourself. Your health is very important. Get to know and understand your body and listen to what it is saying."
—Grace Ferraro

See the good

"My father always instilled in me to see the good in others, even if people may not be so honorable. I learned a lot from being open to people and loving them for who they are. I didn't realize I was learning until I was older because that was just how I was a raised."
—Anonymous

Help others

"At the age of 97, I still ask God what is it that I am supposed to do before I leave this earth and the answer I always come back to is—helping others."
—Thelma Clinard

Daily 5

"Several months ago, I quit a job that I hated. Since then, I have spent a lot of time searching for myself, exploring what I really enjoy in life, acknowledging who I am, and facing insecurities I didn't really know were there. I got used to distracting myself with positive things rather than dealing with what I needed to. Confronting uncomfortable situations brought me to five lessons that I recently learned:

1. I need to be vulnerable, transparent, and open.
2. I need to be thankful, pray, and be joyful.
3. I cannot allow others to dictate how I feel or view myself.
4. I need to know my value and my worth.
5. I am going to be okay."
—Natalie Eloskof

Welcome spirituality

"One time during a retreat, a pastor spoke
to me. I took a seat near the bottom of a
stream and I prayed. During that moment,
something just came over me. That moment
was different and I felt inspired. What crossed
my mind was to help other people. Up until
then, I took church for granted, but when that
happened, I don't know what it was that came
over me like a warm blanket or something.
I often think about that morning and how
different it was. I guess it's good to welcome
spirituality into your life."

—John Ferraiolo

Support is earned when it's given

"If I could share any words of wisdom for others, it would be that our lives aren't as difficult as we make them out to be. When we get in compromising or difficult situations, it's easy to let the brain take the helm and spiral out of control. But when you really break it down, there isn't any situation, or anyone, that can cause a particular feeling. What causes us to feel something is our interpretation of events, people, and circumstances. We create a narrative about how our life is going compared to others or how this particular situation is going to get the best of us. But . . . think about it: this isn't the *first* time you've felt overwhelmed or scared or anxious about something. Aren't you still here? Haven't you overcome those feelings of mediocrity or inferiority or fear before?

You're going to be okay. And if there ever comes a time that you feel like you can't do it alone, there is *always* someone ready to help. Don't be afraid to open up to people. In the end, it's not the things we bought or the career we've built that matters. It's the people we loved and how deeply we loved them that will always remain.

—Kyle Hart

Take it Day by Day

"Do things as they come, day by day. Do all the things that you can today. Tomorrow when you wake up, thank God and continue to do what you've got to do. Do things day by day and *be thankful*. If you have an illness, don't grieve, just take care of it, as a normal human should do. I've had a lot of illness and surgeries. Okay, so listen to me and think about it: do nice things for others. Think of God being by your side. What else can we do?"

—Ann Jean Barbola

A Fortunate Opportunity

"My father was born and raised on the countryside in Eritrea, a third world country in East Africa. He was one of nine children; five of whom passed away before the age of five. Of the remaining four, his only bother was killed in a civil war, and the three sisters were not in the physical shape needed to escape. His sisters' children were also born and raised in Eritrea and are currently struggling to make ends meet. My father eventually escaped the country and was granted entrance into the US as a political refugee. My sister and I were born and raised in Orange County, California. Whenever I feel as though things aren't going well for me in life, whether it is at work or in a relationship, I always reflect on the fact that in the grand scheme of things, I am unbelievably lucky to be granted the life I have. There is always someone out there who is less fortunate than I am. Realizing this helps me appreciate even the littlest of things like vegetables, even though I don't like how they taste."

—Solomon Reda

Be Honest and Be True

"When you are honest and true to who you
are, then your heart will always guide you to
where you want to go."
—Riley Hayes

The Most Important Decision

"The most important decision you will make in your life is not what college you go to, it's who you decide to create a life-long partnership with and have children with. And the reason I say this is because once you bring children into this world, you are locked into a partnership forever. No matter what happens, you will always be responsible for your children and there will always be a tie with the other person."

—Holly Mallick

Good Bye Chuck!

"When I was twenty-four years old, I was diagnosed with an advanced form of thyroid cancer. I don't like the word 'cancer,' so let's use 'Chuck' as a positive replacement. After multiple surgeries and rounds of radiation, my doctor felt there was nothing more that he could do for me. He told me that if I did not find a treatment for my disease, it would overtake my body in about five years. I was in denial arguing with the doctor, shocked, and depressed. During my extensive course of treatment, I relied heavily on others to survive, especially my mother. At one point, over seventy lymph nodes were removed from around my neck, even my jugular vein, which my body naturally grew back on its own. After all the surgeries and procedures, I had limited mobility in my arms. I lost my voice and I was so tired and sore I barely left my bed. During this time, I truly realized the strength and the unconditional love that my mother had for me. Every two hours, she had to give me medications. She woke up in the middle of the night to make sure I was okay and she helped me with everything you can imagine . I felt like her baby again. Fortunately, my relationships grew deeper with everyone: my family, my friends, and even people who I didn't know would send me cards of hope.

I am amazed at how the body heals itself and it makes me really believe in the possibility of a greater being. And although I can't say I have found my purpose, I do feel like everyone has one. And when bad things happen like this, I feel like I go through it so that I can help others through difficult times. I have learned not to take my days for granted and not to be angry with people because I wasted too much time in the past being angry with others. When I go to bed at night, I ask myself, 'If I don't wake up to live tomorrow, am I happy with how my last day went today?' Some days I think, 'Damn, it is not a good time for me to not wake up tomorrow.' I guess you can't have a perfect day every day. One thing is for sure and that is I am not going to let Chuck get the best of me."

—Melissa Gallardo

It may already be in your hand

"Sometimes we think rushing is the best way to ensure our productivity. That's what I thought too. I was on a trip to the Middle East once to conduct research for an upcoming article, and all I could do was think of my deadlines and all the tasks I had to accomplish. I was so caught up with my checklists that I continued to lose opportunities in the moment: opportunities to ask my grandmother about her past or opportunities to get insights from the Bedouins on the streets. I had so much I thought I knew I was going to successfully collect, yet the whole time, what I needed was right in front of me. I soon realized that once I stopped rushing and instead living in the present moment, the infinite quality I was looking for was right in front of me all along."
—Loureen Ayyoub

Comfort and certainty

"Do not sit too comfortably in the seat of certainty."
—Jenny Carraciolo

The simplicity of kindness

"Be kind to everyone. People are already dealing with a lot of hard things. Your one kind act can brighten up someone's hard day."
—Zaif Akhter

What to give your children

"I currently teach a fourth grade cohort of underprivileged, high-risk students. They walked into fourth grade not knowing how to read or solve word problems. Although they may not have been set up with the fundamentals to succeed in their earliest years, I still believe they have the potential to be successful. I have learned that if a child is under stress, it affects their ability to study and memorize, ultimately compromising their ability to learn in school. I have seen the value in the 'fixed mindset, growth mindset' philosophy, by rewarding students for how hard they have worked to accomplish a task rather than simply calling them smart. I want them to realize the value of working hard to accomplish something because those who put effort into their work, succeed in life. I also try to teach them to be nice people and realize they are still so fortunate and capable. I remember one day I wore an old pair of shoes to school and my students made fun of me.

I said to them, 'I only wear shoes to protect my feet, I don't care what they look like.' I tried to help them realize that, last night, they slept in their beds at home, got dressed this morning, and made it to school, as compared to other children in the world who do not have that opportunity. I want them to understand that there are many people who are worse off than they, and that even though they, too, are in a tough situation, they have the ability to make a positive difference. At the end of the day, however, there is one thing remains true, which is that all children need and want to be successful in school and in life. My one piece of advice is to all parents: make sure your children feel loved and cared for and make it known that you are proud of them. At ten-years-old, I don't think anything is your fault."

—Alexandria Whitmer

Be diligent with your relationships

"I've learned that momentum in a relationship emits passion. Stay diligent in your relationships. Consistently make delicate adjustments so you stay in sync. But only if you want to."
—Hilary Polley

The world will reciprocate

"No one is in charge of your happiness but yourself. Put good energy into the universe and good will come back to you. Love always prevails."
—Angela Juarez

Use rejection and failure as fuel

"Being oppressed in the medical field, despite my resume and educational degrees, I continue to feel motivated. The reason being, I used this rejection as fuel to pursue further development to open more opportunities. Rejection and failure don't always mean you failed, it may be a stepping stone to improving yourself and capitalizing from your mistakes."
—Anthony Gil

Embracing Now

"Be mindful and always embrace the current moment. Never look back or too far ahead."
—Kira Nashed

Mistakes make you wiser

"Wisdom is expressed in so many ways. Someone might be wise to deal with something but may not be wise to deal with other things. Wisdom is something that is acquired throughout the years and with certain life experiences and obstacles. We may not always find a solution and sometimes we make matters worse but in order to get wiser, we must make mistakes."
—Ramiro Guillan

Don't hide your gift

"There's nothing 'ordinary' about any person or their life. Every individual has an incredible chance to be extraordinary—some just refuse to take it while others refuse to believe it. It's far too easy to be a follower and blend in with the cattle, while it's much more rewarding to stand out and carve your own path in life. I used to think that to be extraordinary, I would have to be an 'alpha' character or become someone of dominance over others. Boy, was I wrong. To be extraordinary is to inspire. To inspire is to let others see through you into something larger. It's allowing yourself to shine your own light brighter than to find room under someone else's beam. It's being vulnerable in a world flooded with shame. Most of all, it's knowing that your boundaries are truly a figment of your imagination. Inspiration comes in many forms, but it has these common denominators. It means being the truest form of yourself and embracing what you bring to the world. It's having endless opportunities to make a positive impact on others—which all starts within yourself. We live in a world where self-betterment is more underrated than ever. We're taught to look for happiness in materials and relationships with others while neglecting ourselves and underrating our self-worth. Every single one of us in our true form is truly gifted with dreams of making a difference. It's only up to you what you do with your extraordinary gift. Don't hide it from the world."

—Ramez Bishara

Share your knowledge in a positive and loving light

"Wisdom is unique to each individual. You gain wisdom not only through your own trials and tribulations, but also from the experiences others share with you. When I think of wisdom, something might come to mind that wouldn't come to the mind of others. The wisdom I have gained over the years has shaped and modeled my actions. To spread my wisdom onto others would still be unique to each individual based on their interpretation. However, the one thing that stays consistent is how I share it. I share it with love and the intention to better this Earth while glorifying God. I love to believe that if one spreads knowledge in a positive and loving light, it will provide others with the insight they need to gain their own wisdom. Perhaps I am presenting the idea that true wisdom comes from the ability to take your experiences in life and share it in a positive way. But that's just my idea."

—Robert Patton

Spirituality, Passion, and Hard Work

"I immigrated to the US when I was only nineteen years old. Considering my culture shock and lack of life experiences, I shouldn't have succeeded in this country. However, my spiritual faith, along with a passion for education and strong belief that hard work pays off, I managed to succeed as an immigrant who came to the US with nothing. I give credit to so many teachers who saw my shortcomings, but knew my potential even when I didn't."

—Saba Reda

Stick up for yourself and be nice to people

"I always tell my daughter, 'Defend yourself and others.' Also, to 'Always be kind to others.'"
—Lorena Cabrera

Love, learn, and grow

"My scars are my trophies. My mistakes are my lessons. My flaws are beautiful even if I'm still working on seeing the beauty within myself. Life is a balance of learning what we can and cannot control. I've learned to always stay true to the person I am. Choose people who will love and support you and continue to be around through good and bad. Life is all about loving, learning, and growing."
—Michelle Rosenlund

You are strong & beautiful

"Love yourself and live your life with no regrets. Realize that every experience, no matter how good or bad, has shaped you into who you are today. You are strong and you are beautiful."

—Jennifer White

Be good to everyone you meet

"You never know when you may meet someone who can be a connection or of service to you in the future. So choose your friends wisely. An enemy today could become a friend in the future and vice versa. Peace, love, and blessings to all."
—Thomas Webster

Only you should define who you are

"If you let other people define who you are then you aren't living your life and you aren't finding your purpose. If you let other people define who you are, you are agreeing to put them in control of you."
—Lucero Hernandez

Be open

"People are better than we are inclined to believe. If you are going through something hard, don't close yourself off from others. Chances are, they can offer what you need for healing."
—Kelly Valenzuela

Listen to understand

"Greed is the enemy of good. Don't fight to get a whole loaf of bread if half of it will keep you moving forward. You can always come back later for the rest of the loaf, if it's really that important. Usually, it isn't. Also, I have learned that it is important to listen to other people to *understand* what they mean by what they say. What we hear isn't always what is meant. Repeat back to them how you understood they said and they will thank you for that."
—David Kay

First, love yourself

"Love yourself first. Never doubt your abilities and don't stop trying until you get to where you are meant to be."
—Stephanie Lopez

Think for yourself

"Think for yourself. Don't allow social media to do it for you. Enjoy the time that you have with your friends and family. Travel the world while you can. Don't spend so much time looking at what other people are doing with their life and instead focus on yours and enjoy it while you can."
—Ricardo Montes

Kevin's Five Notes of Wisdom

"1. Never take 'no' for an answer if you are trying to achieve your dreams. If you fail, figure out another way to accomplish it.
2. Never lose the opportunity to tell someone how you feel. That feeling of regret will eat away at you.
3. Don't be afraid to tell a stranger they are beautiful.
4. Never let anyone tell you that you can't make it. Stick to what you want and continue to pursue your dreams.
5. Be honest and be genuine . . . Don't be too quick to judge someone; you don't know what they are going through."

—Kevin Young

Give thanks in remembrance

"1. Give thanks in remembrance; A farmer cannot produce crop by simply planting seeds. Just because a farmer cultivates and works hard, it doesn't mean he collects crop. The sun must shine, a bit of wind, and with the help of the rain, the farmer has a chance to produce and collect the crops he planted. Similarly, in life, the Lord needs to give blessings in order for one to receive and multiply. Thinking deeply helps us to remember our blessings.

2. Give thanks by sharing: When an individual receives and acknowledges a blessing, it should naturally overflow, leaving some to share with others. Be selfless and share.

3. Give thanks with dedication: Your dedication may guide others to be motivated. So give thanks joyfully. Rejoice always, pray continually, give thanks in all circumstances for it is God's will for you."
—Tony Shin

I can do all through Christ

"I am a young female who was raised in the church, so I have very strong Christian beliefs. My favorite bible verse I live by each day is Philippians 4:13 which states, 'I can do all things through Christ who strengthens me.' As a former athlete, a current student, and employee just going through everyday life, we learn that we are put through hard times, having unfortunate events happen. But no matter the circumstances, or how hard it may get, God will always push us through. He is my strength who pushes and motivates me to reach my goals daily."

—Synclaire Hamilton

Nothing is more valuable than health

"My life flipped upside down when my mother, who I love more than life itself, was diagnosed with breast cancer. I was nineteen years old and I was terrified. I remember so vividly pacing in the hospital while she was having surgery to have the tumor removed. The surgery took several hours. As I walked back and forth from the car to the lobby, and then back to the car and then back to the lobby, I looked up at the sky and begged for the universe to let me keep my mom. Luckily, they caught the disease early on and she fully recovered. I did learn an invaluable lesson from the process, which is that life is really, really great as long as you and your loved ones are healthy. There is nothing more valuable than health and as long as you're in a healthy state nothing else can really be that bad."

—Zoya Biglary

Respect the world

"Respect the world. Just because you are intelligent, it doesn't mean that you know everything. Often times, wisdom comes with age."
—Penny Jung

Family first

"Heart transplants for both my husband and I brought us closer than ever before. It made us realize that our family was more important than money and traveling and such. It gave us a different perspective on life. It made us realize that family was more important and that we wanted to be closer to them . . . We felt that if we lived through this, that if we survive this, it was meant to be and we would help others. It gave me the perspective that you are not on this planet for just any reason. Everybody has a reason to be here and they have to make the best. [My] source of strength was daily prayer."

—Sandra Landan

Family is what's important

"I have always believed that family is not the most important part of my life, it is the *only* important part of my life. Life is not complicated, but sometimes we make it so. We can enjoy every single minute of it if we keep it simple. After all, life is what we make of it."

—Sal Salceda

Trust your gut

"Trust yourself. You know more than you think
you do. Intuition is real and you don't have to be a
mother to feel it. A sense of personal peace should
always be your reference point when taking the next
steps in your life."
—Siana Ayyoub

Don't be impulsive

"Never make a decision when you are angry,
and never take shortcuts on your journey."
—Cesar Ortiz

Focus on what is yours

"Don't compare your marriage to other marriages.
And don't compare your kids to other kids. Stay
focused on what is yours."
—Mike R. Smith

Success is best when shared

"Success is such a common word but means so many different things to people. My definition of success is very simple—it means being able to share my time with my family, in peace. Being able to share experiences and go through life together as a family, and not let other people interfere with my family's upbringing. I feel so fortunate to not worry about things such as food, or having gas in my car. I feel like successful people share their wisdom with the people they surround themselves with, and as a result, they become successful too. It's a way of life. It's a way to grow as a community. When you grow individually it's not as fun or rewarding or beneficial for your community. But if you grow as a team and rise together, the journey to success makes so much more sense. I can see my success in the future developing through my family, friends, and community. Success is best when shared."

—Jake Onorato

Be respectful and loyal

"Respect and loyalty are the key to happiness. Respect others around you and you will get the same respect in return. Loyalty to your loved ones is everything."
—Magtanggol Dawil

Set boundaries and limits early on

"God gave you a brain to use. Don't let people take advantage of you. Learn to set boundaries and limits early on. Do not let the world deceive you, and remember that love is based on action and not just the simplicity of words."
—Anna Ayyoub

How you are remembered

"The greatest asset of character is how you're remembered by others when you're not in their presence. After all, the impressions you've left and how you're remembered is what counts."
—Zaren Chiranian

No regrets allowed

"Never have any regrets, no matter what it is. We make decisions without always knowing what the outcome will be. And, at one point, it may have been what we wanted. Live life with no regrets, you will be happy and prosperous."
—Cristian Castro

Start early

"Always wake up before the sunrise."
—Shawn Ortiz

Be helpful, not hurtful

"Always try to be helpful, but if you can't, then
don't be hurtful. Put yourself in the other
person's shoes."
—Marc Gonzales

Surround yourself with those who can add the right ingredients to your life

"It is interesting to know someone who sees you not only as the person you are, but also as the person who you can become. My wife does this daily. Since the day I met her she has always seen past my imperfections. Using an awesome fruit analogy: She picked up a banana that had some brown spots. A banana that may have been dropped in its past and overlooked by others, but was still edible to a degree. She didn't just see a banana that was bruised. She saw more, an ingredient to something greater. By adding some sweet elements of her own, the love she has been shown by a Savior, the leaven of life experiences, meanwhile, maintaining the original and unique flavor of the banana, she has created something superior. She has turned me into something greater: Banana Bread. Surround yourself with people who do this. If it is a spouse, you're lucky."

—Drake Fages

Learn to work hard early

"I am the oldest of eight children. When we were young, our father always gave us tasks that seemed ridiculous, long, and laborious. For example, we would pick stones from our field and water an acre of tomato plants, one by one. When I was an adult he told me that he gave us those tasks so that we could learn to work together. We were always together and we worked a lot. Now we are all adults and have grown to become an amazing family. My dad passed at fifty-three and his children have held strong. Looking back, what I learned from this is that children need chores; they need to learn to work together with no allowance. This is the responsibility of family. Learn it, love it, and grow from it. Work hard to become a stronger person, be a problem solver, and learn to lead."

—Meghan Shigo

Judging and righteous judgment

"Most people are familiar with the saying 'Judge not and Ye shall not be judged.' But there is also a compliment to that saying that invokes quite an interesting thought: 'Ye must judge righteous Judgment.' The common thread between the two thoughts is the decision one is faced with. Does one not judge another because one is in fear of being judged? Or does one judge what another is doing as righteous or not? This is a balance that each of us experience almost daily, as we walk together in life. Balancing the experience we have with one another is what we all look back upon as the day closes. What we think about these experiences reveals what we think about the person."

—Martin Vasquez

Speak life into people

"Let your light be so bright that it radiates and breaks though the darkness. Do not underestimate the power of a smile and a kind word. Let your tongue only speak life into people. Some quarrels just aren't worth the effort. Time is your most precious asset, don't lose it on empty things."
—Jacqueline Isaac

If life were perfect, there would be no reason to hope

"Inspiration comes from letting life in and experiencing things and situations for what they truly are. In return, life will inspire one to be or to do. Stick to your decisions until the cycle is complete, even when you are unsure of what the end looks like or means. Experience life by taking a few steps back for a greater perspective. Attempt to let situations, words, thoughts, or whatever it may be, marinate before acting or speaking. The more I practice this method, the more informed I become regarding what to allow into my life. When you are in the thick of things and on autopilot, not much sinks in. Hence, you don't really get to wholly experience that moment. I try to live by speaking, listening, and viewing the world through a universal language taking in the music, the colors, and the love that is within reach.

Our world is perfectly balanced. Everything and everyone has a yin to its yang. People say life is hard, or a shipwreck headed nowhere. But then again, that is why it is beautiful. Because of this, you have the opportunity to feel hope with something to look forward to. The concept of a glass being half-filled or empty is great, but I've always been the type of person who didn't care to see the glass. I like to think that it is neither empty nor full. It's simply what I believe it is. What you say or do enough of, will eventually be."
—Sharifa Muhammad

You never know what you can mean to someone

"I was in an abusive relationship for two years and when I finally decided to leave, I found myself in a deep depression. I felt that I had no self-worth and was alone. I attended church and my spiritual life grew, but I still continued to feel alone. People would ask if I was okay as if they were saying, 'Hello' or 'Good morning.' After experiencing depression for about six months, I realized that I kept giving people surface kind of answers. I finally decided to start letting people know exactly how I was feeling and what I was going through, whether or not they truly intended to know. I allowed myself to be vulnerable and express more about what I was experiencing. Once I did this, people started to offer their help or a listening ear. Later, I went on a three-month road trip around the US. Normally I would sit and wait at a stop by myself, but on this particular day, I decided to sit near a girl who was diligently writing in her journal. When

I noticed she had stopped writing, I asked what she was writing about. I had zero intention to talk to anybody. She looked at me and began to talk about how alone she felt, how the most important relationship in her life had ended and she felt lost. It felt like a reiteration of my exact story. She was struggling with depression. She eventually turned the journal towards me and allowed me to read her entry for the day. We decided not to treat each other as strangers. We let each other in and allowed ourselves to become vulnerable. She joined us the rest of the day on our hikes and into a freezing plunge into the lake with the highest altitude in the USA. She talked about everything that was running through her mind. You never know what you could mean to another person. You never know if you could be that listening ear they need. Everybody will be a stranger to you until you decide to treat him or her as a friend."

—Alberto Sanchez

Do not let bitterness distract you from your hopes

"I do not feel safe in the neighborhood I live in because there is a popular unjust perception of people who look like me. As valid as my feelings concerning my safety are, I will not allow myself to become bitter. This is my hope and my choice.

I do not have a criminal record but ironically, I have been forcefully detained twice within the last three months for fitting the description of a suspect in the area. I am often afraid of what will happen to me when I leave my home. All my friends who look like me have similar stories of how they've also been racially profiled, violated, and humiliated by the government force sworn to protect and serve us.

We speak openly with one another. We listen without diminishing the value of each other's experiences. We consider other marginalized communities and minority groups, who have also felt helplessness in a similar way that I feel now. It is my responsibility to remember that as much as I need their support, they also need mine. It is my right as an American citizen to speak out on behalf of the disenfranchised. It is my privilege to stand with them in demand of equity and equality. While anger is a healthy response to injustice, bitterness distracts from hope.

No one should ever have to stand alone. There are too many unfortunate biases that exist in the world today, creating caste systems that benefit some but oppress others. Racial profiling is a systemic issue that impacts many people of color. My hope is for a world without the hateful 'isms.' I want a healthier society for the next generation supported by the choices that we make now to effectively solve the problems that plague our nation. Though it feels impossible, this is the hope that I choose."

—Isaiah Smith

Your purpose should always trump your fears

"'Life is short.' It's a phrase that most of us take for granted. A phrase that can be taken lightly when you have a seemingly endless amount of time ahead of you. It wasn't until I witnessed death that I understood the power behind such a simple phrase. Nowadays, it is easy to get swept up in society's expectations. It's easy to follow a routine and get stuck in it, to feel like you're missing out on your purpose, while not having the control to govern the direction your life should move in—to feel like you don't control your destiny. Your family, your environment, and your world control it.

I have felt this way before. I have felt pressure, even if it was self-inflicted. Doubtful thoughts, depression, or anxiety can follow you when you try to go against the grain.

But the moment I witnessed my father take his last breath was the moment I realized that one's purpose should always trump their fears. A life with purpose is a life worth living. The passion that burns deep in you is your calling. Hold onto it. Try to fulfill it as much as you can.

In that moment of tragedy, I learned to live so that when my time comes, I will have as little regret as I could fight off. Because, as we all know, life is short."
—Jeremy Crooks

God's wishes are above all

"I tried so hard to get into dental school. I had a good GPA, strong DAT scores, volunteer experience, and you name it. I tried for three years and still was not accepted. Finally someone advised me to give pharmacy school a shot, so I did. I applied one week before the deadline and received two acceptance letters. My dad told me something may have gone wrong if I were to become a dentist and that this is God's way of helping me avoid that."
—Mina Guirguis

You have a future

"As long as you are alive, you have a future."
—Susan Geffen

Don't confuse wants and needs

"I learned that our language causes perpetual disorganization. We use the word 'need' instead of 'want' for everything. We are afraid to want. We 'need' everything. We say 'I need to go to the store,' 'I need to pick up the kids,' 'I need new shoes.' It's a trick we play on our subconscious process, a lie in essence to justify overdoing it, collecting, and accumulation. We only need air, food, water, sleep, shelter, elimination, and sunlight—the seven things that keep us alive. Everything else is a want or don't want, will or won't. We want to regain our use of want and will for everything except the seven essential things in life, the things we need the most."
—Marla Stone

Check your baggage & perspective

"The most important lesson I have learned is that the other person's baggage is not my issue. Also, stop being afraid of what could go wrong and start being positive about what could go right."
—Lauren Spiglanin

Advice from an 8-year-old

"Be nice to people and give money to the poor."
—Jasmine Aguilar

It is never too late to build yourself up again

"The most difficult time in my life was when we lost everything and the market crashed. We had to file for bankruptcy, our cars were repossessed, and we even lost our home. At that moment in time, I never thought we would come back up. But together, we learned to save our money and build ourselves back up again."
—Lidia Fransis

An anonymous letter that showed up at my doorstep
The ugly side of love

"We all experience love and know what love is. Unfortunately, I didn't think there could be a different side to such a beautiful feeling but I just recently found the ugly side of love.

I found my husband of fifteen years going behind me and engaging in communication with other women. A-not-so-apologetic apology ensued when I confronted him after seeing the content in his phone. If he claims he loves me, why would he do all that?

I don't know and can't answer for him, but I will say that despite all of my hurt and pain, I still love him. I've learned that love isn't about happy thoughts and beautiful images all the time. There can be an ugly side to it. A side where one's heart and soul become so damaged that it can become difficult to trust. I will continue to live my life with a smile on my face. My friends and family may never know of the pain I experience inside. This isn't a sympathy letter or seeking advice or counseling. I know you are writing a book and wanted to share this perspective."

—Anonymous

Easy

"Your parents are your parents and that's it. The people who made you might not be the best mentors, and it's not fair to depend on them for your happiness. Observe and learn from many other adults throughout your adolescence. Take with you what you like and leave the rest. Learn how you want or don't want to live your life. Create your own family tree. What you do in your 20s really does matter and it will set the tone for your future. Do not wait until your 30s or 40s to start thinking about getting out of debt, starting a career, or whom you will marry. Start thinking about it when you can, and start making moves in the direction of your goals. The story you tell yourself about your life, who you date, where you work, and those whom you surround yourself with will ultimately shape the rest of your life.

People change, and it's okay to let go of toxic individuals. Just separate yourself from them in a kind way. Experience life to the fullest, but stay grounded. And know that addiction to things, as well as people, can be dangerous. So strive for balance and moderation in all things. I don't recommend borrowing or lending money to family members. Unearned vacations you put on credit cards instead of saving up for them is simply irresponsible living and will only bring guilt and stress. Live and let live. We cannot fix or change people. Those individuals we want to 'fix' must make their own life choices. Set a good example and treat everyone the way you want to be treated, even on a bad day. And remember smiles are contagious."
—Channel Rivers

Living positively in the moment

"In this fast-paced life, it can be easy to take our blessings for granted. Something so simple as the breath in our body can be overlooked. Life is a beautiful thing and I cannot stress how imperative it is to enjoy the blessings we are surrounded by.

I want you to take a moment from reading this and look around you. Take a deep breath in and exhale any negative energy or stress that you may be carrying. In this moment, clear your mind, take in the natural beauty, appreciate the daily activities of life happening before your eyes, and realize how fortunate you are.

Now that we have cleansed our minds, let me share a personal story and one of my biggest sources of inspiration. My cousin has battled cystic fibrosis his whole life and recently was given a new lease on life. He went into lung failure and was blessed with a guardian angel in the form of a donor. He received a double lung transplant after pushing the limits of life support. I spent a lot of time on the transplant wing in the hospital and got to know families who were patiently waiting for the renewal of their loved one's life. Many of these families did not know if this was the last time they were going to see their loved one. I stepped back and just appreciated the palpable love that was in the waiting room of the transplant wing. Throughout his journey, I realized the importance of not letting daily distractions clutter my mind and appreciating some of the greater things in life.

My cousin demonstrated to me the importance of taking a breath! It may sound obvious, but to someone who has struggled his whole life to simply oxygenate himself, it should not be taken for granted. So next time you're having a bad day, step back, take a deep breath, look outside, and know that there are people out there that love you dearly and will be there for you until the end. Don't let daily irritants distract you from this blessing that is life!"

—Chris Paul

Health is vital

"Your health is vital. It affects your body, mind, and soul. Make the best of your time, as it will pass you by. Dream big. Make your goals measurable and attainable."
—Mario James

Happiness is . . .

"You know, I think happiness is a byproduct of the way you live, which is displayed in your attitude. If you see the glass as half-empty, you aren't going to be as happy as if you see it half-full. The people who see it as half-empty are often very hard to be around. Life is about relationships; it's not about stuff. Some people have more stuff but happiness from that is not something that lasts. I think it's important to see that there are people who have a lot in life yet are not grateful for what they have. Other people aren't happy at all and they have a whole bunch of stuff. They always want more, and they usually aren't very happy. If I could offer any words of wisdom, it would be to try and help other people and be grateful for the things that you have. Don't think about what you don't have. You can drive yourself crazy—just be grateful for what you do have."

—Anonymous

Get to know you

"This world is full of people who don't quite take the time to fully understand themselves and try to work out pieces of a puzzle that they don't even have all the parts to. Moving in this manner is basically like giving advice when you haven't experienced a thing close to what you're giving advice about. Take time to see the bigger picture not only from what's around you, but more importantly from what's inside you. Hopefully you will find someone you can be proud of."

—Daniel Rockbank

Fight your fears

"So many of us fall into the nature of just living life, but are we truly living? Often times, we mask our bad habits and actions so we don't have to deal with our problems. We unknowingly continue to sink into those habits thinking we are running away from the problem. But problems will always stay and/or get worse when ignored. We have the power to decide if a problem will be fixed. No one else can fix it. Yes, it can be scary, but beating fear requires going towards that unknown that fear loves to lurk in. Once you approach your fears, the light will start to shine through. A twinkling met by brighter and brighter light until . . . Success! Fear has nowhere to hide in the light. It may linger a bit, but more and more, fear will be brightened by the light and will not survive. Yes, there is a light at the tunnel—don't be afraid to see it."

—Rebekah Youssefi

Pray for strength

"My whole life, I have struggled with my illness. I have seen it go from bad to worse but through it all, I know God is with me. I believe we are all equipped with strength, and it takes an illness or a reason to beat the odds to bring it out. My faith is a big part of my strength. A nurse told me a great quote, 'Strength is fear that has said its prayers.' So no matter how many hurdles you have to go over, pray that God will give you the strength and know he will be with you."

—Tina Nasre

The past is history

"Don't bring an old suitcase to a new location. Every new season is meant for a fresh start and a clean slate. The past is history and today is yours to keep."
—Maggie Barsoum

Bring people together

"They say, 'Travel is food for the soul' and this never made more sense to me than during my own personal experiences in France and Morocco. As a young Muslim college student, I was always trying to find ways to accomplish my prayer rituals. As part of a student TV organization, I was at a racing tournament in Corsica, camping in the mountains. As I was looking for a quiet area, I came across the owner of the camp who asked me what I was doing. To my surprise, he opened his house to me and left me alone in his living room. I felt safe and protected, free to accomplish my daily prayer. This man trusted me with all of his belongings though he had barely met me. What enlightened me even more was that this man was Christian.

Another unforgettable instance occurred as I was interning on a film set. I walked out and realized I was in a fairly dangerous neighborhood. I asked someone if they knew of any quiet place nearby where I could pray. Although this gentleman was headed to work, he smiled and led me to his family's apartment. They welcomed me with tea and cookies.

These moments were eye-opening to me because in both cases, religion was what connected me to these people. Neither race nor skin, simply religion. This is often a negative subject of discussion, yet here I was, welcomed by Muslims and non-Muslims alike into their own homes all because we mutually shared the same passion for our common divine entity.

I wanted to share this story to remind others that regardless of what we may hear, religion should always remain what its Latin root actually means, 'religare.' Religare is defined as, 'bringing people together' and nothing else."
—Aziz Tazi

Success comes from other people

"Always sell yourself and make an impression because you never know who is listening.

All my success comes from other people: meeting new people, networking, and always seeking new opportunities. You have to just keep going. I do not let obstacles dictate my life. I continue to knock on doors. Anywhere and everywhere, I give out my business card and say, 'Hey, let's do something.' Some of my best connections came from other people who were just starting out like me.

My success comes from just being out there and being exposed. Even if you think it has nothing to do with what you're doing right now, you never know. I think what helped me in my first year of success was being exposed to anything. People tend to get stressed about rules, others judging them, or people getting upset with them.

Things come and go.
People come and go.
Opportunities come and go.
So be open to anything.

I knew what I wanted to create and I was going to
keep working until I made it a reality. Reinventing
yourself is important because changes are constantly
happening around you. We cannot stay stagnant in
our ways if the world is changing around us."
—Alejandra Viana

Enjoy fearlessly

"I think one of the most important things I have learned, and am still learning, is patience. We tend to be very eager and hungry to know our whole future right away, so we overthink it. And when we do that, we create so much stress for ourselves. Then every bump in the road tends to bring us anxiety and fear, but the truth is, everything happens when it needs to happen and where we are is where we need to be. Stressing over it won't make anything unfold faster. So why not enjoy the process fearlessly, while waiting patiently for the puzzle to be complete?"
—Carla Kechichian

**The most important lessons
I have learned are that . . .**

"Life is short so it's important to embrace
every moment of your journey. Be present.
Love fiercely. Embrace conversations and every
person you encounter like it would be your
last. Exercise. Be creative and don't be afraid
to share your creation. Ask questions, take
chances, and don't be afraid to fail. Learn from
your mistakes. Know your worth and let go of
what doesn't make you happy. And don't forget
that there is always room to grow and learn.
Learn to laugh at yourself and compliment
others."
—John Fransis

The power of biblical meditation

"The true source of wisdom comes from a realm beyond man's wildest imagination and comprehension. We have the ability to tap into this realm through various sources, including biblical and revelation meditation.

As spiritual, physical, and emotional beings, we are called to seek the wisdom of this realm. Biblical meditation incorporates extracting various scriptures and meditating on them, with the eyes open or closed. Ideally, the scriptures are short, sweet, and relevant to what we are going through in life at that juncture. When we close our eyes and enter into the realm of infinite possibilities, we must invite God's Holy Spirit to fill us with wisdom and revelation, guiding us in our lives and the path we walk.

If you find that this is hard to fathom, I can understand. My personal walk in the meditation world started through eastern meditation techniques, as well as deep yoga and other forms of meditation and physical well-being. However, this led me to a place I did not expect, which was an encounter with the Holy Spirit of Jesus Christ.

I realized that when I had this experience, I had to end my old way of meditation and learn a new way. What I learned is that meditating actively on the Word of God is much more powerful than any form of eastern meditation technique. Also, we can meditate this way anywhere we find ourselves throughout the day, and even walking with our eyes open, or driving the car. I have found that there is an infinitely greater level and depth of revelation and wisdom in this form of mediation.

If you are interested in spirituality (but not religiosity), then this form of biblical and revelation meditations are for you."
—Eduardo Espirito Santo

Keep close to God

"Be conscious of the present. Do not always be in a hurry, anxious, or impatient, for these things can potentially make you miss the real present. Focus on what He has already done for you and what He has placed in front of you. Center your troubles, worries, and doubts on your creator who has determined your destiny. Tune into the spiritual realm by being still, opening your soul to our savior, and asking Him to reveal your purpose. Keep close to God and he will remove your worries and replace them with perseverance."

—Genesis Garcia

Don't take life too seriously

"Don't take life too seriously; I feel like we all get so caught up with work and other things that may not matter in the big picture, and ultimately we miss out on the things that matter, like time with family. To this day, this is still something I am working on."
—Nicole Sanders

Love is God's favorite religion

"We need a reliable system that can offer equal opportunities to all, away from the greedy, fake rhetoric geographical boundaries we set as global citizens of different nations. We all belong to one planet, in one world and live under one sky. Pollution doesn't differentiate between a Chinese and an American, cancer doesn't differentiate between an African and an Arab, just like poverty doesn't differentiate between a South American and an Australian.

Love is God's favorite religion, but if our genes as humans are Asian, Turkish, Persian, British, or of any origin, it won't make a difference as long as pollution, poverty, and violence are a result of those same genes which made the globe today a more brutal one.

We need to manage the world ecosystem, not empty political seminars. We need armies and missiles with more faith and less religion, we need technology that can preserve our roots and not make our lifetime a virtual one. What the world needs today is not to let the fast eat the slow, nor the big to end the small but to manage the fast until the slow becomes a part of the fast, and grow the small until the small becomes a part of the big. The process should allow all individuals a share of the market. In order to do that, we must prelude the idea that the air, oceans and trees and everything else we share as humans, has only one religion."

—Samer Kabbara

Success is within reach

"The key to success is first knowing that success is within reach. After you fully believe that, nothing can stop you."
—Trevor Nguyen

Always find the best

"All this stuff is called living . . . Some people learn to enjoy it, some people fight it. Whoever sets the clock up there in the celestial factory, you know, every once in a while they goof and someone doesn't do it right . . . They made this beautiful planet, they put the water there, and everything else, and then turned to an apprentice angel and said, 'There it is, now take care of it.' This poor angel didn't know what he was doing. Now look at the result. Look at how many churches and how many houses of religions that we have just in this country. And we do more killing of people just because of what church they go to than for any other reason. What I would say, is to always try to find the best in a person when you meet them. Do not judge them in the beginning because people give false impressions. There will always be a grouch, someone to impress you, and someone to complain."

—Sandy Kaplan

Focus on what will make a mark

"Life is very short and there are too many things to do before it ends. If one day everything will be gone and forgotten, why worry so much about little disruptions? Instead, focus on the things that will make a mark. Personally, I would rather look back at the way I lived and be able to have pride in the fact that I did everything I possibly could to have a superlative life!"
—Lael Mindes

Happiness requires effort

"The most important lesson in life I have learned is to always be in the process of attaining happiness. Happiness is a constant process that you have to work toward."
—Tiara Klugherz

Do what brings you joy.
Stress less and live more.

"The most important lesson I have learned is to pursue what brings you joy. I have been an athlete and dreamed of being an Olympian since I was four years old. Competing brought me joy for twenty-five years, and as soon as I realized I would be just shy of reaching the Olympics in 2016 my joy for competition ended. I was still training and racing as a professional cyclist, but had no real direction or purpose. Just before this, I was invited to race in a Six Day race in Europe, which had a DJ, huge light shows, and upwards of 15,000 people a night drinking, partying, and having a great time. With no real pressure to get huge results during the race, I focused my energies on entertaining the crowds and interacting with the fans. I felt like a rock star! People around the world said I was what Six Day racing had been missing. My joy had been found again; I had a whole new outlook and joy. I may not get as many wins as the current world and Olympic champions, but I am sure to be a crowd favorite!

If I could offer words of wisdom to benefit others, it would be stress less and live more. What I learned through competing in different sports was that how I dealt with the ending of one event would carry over to the next. I had a choice. I could be angry, upset, and frustrated about how an event turned out, or I could accept it and move on and make the very best out of the next event. It is amazing how well this works in real life situations like getting a speeding ticket, being tight on finances, or not getting a job you applied for. The stress will linger and affect your next life event. The sooner it can be accepted, the better chances your next 'event' will have."
—Nate Koch

Keep the ride going

"When I was a young boy, my father, brother, and I rode our bikes together every Saturday morning. We would venture on a five-mile round trip through the neighborhoods and streets of Los Angeles. When I was thirteen, my father passed away and I felt like the world had abandoned me. I continued to ride my bike in remembrance of him on Saturdays and then I found myself riding every single day. I am now a Professional BMX Rider, Entrepreneur, and YouTuber. I average 60,000 views per day and my fans tell me that my content brings them joy. I think that my father would be proud of the impact I have had on others. In honor of those you love, keep the ride going."

—Alfredo Mancuso

Strive to be good

"Strive to always be a good person. This will make the world a better place. I think this world would benefit from having more good people around; people who take care of the world and each other."

—Carmen Boyer

Forgiveness and freedom

"'You can't start the next chapter of your life if you keep rereading the last one,' is a quote which resonates deeply with me. Life can be complicated, and as you live, you become more aware of your imperfections and your failures. It's easy to look back and wish that you did things differently. I have learned that life and happiness are about moving forward. It is important to embrace your past, but not to let it define you. Freedom comes from accepting where you came from, learning from your journey, and choosing joy on a daily basis. You will never regret loving too much, forgiving even when it is not deserved, or giving people the benefit of the doubt. I have learned to consistently focus on the blessings in my life and find ways to be a blessing in others' lives. Never take anything for granted! If you choose to be positive, your failures can be a gift that you never knew you needed."
—Maraya Hardy

Be the best you

"Always be the best you. Be nice to everyone. You never know who can help you get to where you want to be in life. I am friends with everyone, even my competitors at work, and it has lead me to other job opportunities. You never know who is watching. Also, don't take life too seriously."
—Evan Taylor

Narrow down what makes you happy

"One incredibly important lesson that I seem to learn more as life progresses, is the importance of unconditional support of your friends and family. This comes in many forms, and can't be generalized into doing A, B, C, or D. Rather, being aware, conscious, and sensitive to others' needs regarding their dreams, deepest fears, and sincerest concerns. It means listening first and speaking your mind second. It means dropping something on your agenda to hear a friend through a tough time or talk them through their biggest dreams. It's attending the charity softball game that your friend organized even though he didn't come to your last BBQ.

To me, support is unconditional, and should be given liberally until that privilege is taken for granted. I think we quickly forget that we're all in this mess together, whether we like it or not.

I think happiness is doing at least one thing you truly love every day and being aware of it. Even if it's fifteen minutes to sew, or an hour pumping iron at the gym, it's important to narrow down what makes you *feel* happy. I think the first step is not finding what that is for you, but rather understanding what happiness feels like in the moment. People come to that realization at different times in life. No matter what it means for you, you have to understand it first. If you haven't found it yet, it's never too late to do so. How quickly people forget that we pretty much always still have time."

—Kyle Hart

Don't think about what you didn't do in your life

"In 2002, I learned that I had testicular cancer. I had surgery and twenty-five sessions of intensive radiation treatments. Two years later, I found it had spread to my chest, formed a large tumor that was squeezing my aorta and esophagus, and it was going to kill me soon unless I immediately started chemotherapy treatment, though there was still no guarantee of surviving it.

Instead of thinking of all the things I didn't do in my life, facing death presented a great opportunity to reflect on doing whatever it took to stick around to see my sons grow up, and that I would allow fate to decide what I would do to repay for another chance at life.

Now, I don't know for sure about the purpose of life, but I do know that I wanted to make sure my family was always taken care of and given the best life I could provide. In the past I believed that, in order to achieve this, it required working long hours and weekends devoted to my job, to the detriment of family time. That thought completely changed after fighting cancer. I want to see my wife happy, and show attention and interest in what my children have chosen for their career paths.

The most important lesson I have learned is that you can't go back and change how you lived, you can't take back words you wish you had never said, and there is no rewinding days to do over what you should have done in the first place. Make sure events from today and tomorrow don't pile on to your list of regrets. And also, be thankful when you are given the second chance to be a better person."
—John Stephen Phillips

Reflection

When I made the decision to explore wisdom, I became energized and excited at what I would uncover. The motivation for this project started as a quest for personal growth to ascribe more meaning and value to every moment of the day. I was eager to hear stories that would inspire me for personal guidance and growth, but I was also looking forward to sharing my findings with others.

The birth of this project started many years ago, when I was writing my thesis for graduate school about the study of wisdom. Initially, I was interviewing older adults but have expanded my population after learning that wisdom is not necessarily an age-related characteristic. As I was nearing the end and trying to gather my thoughts on what I learned about wisdom, my imagination suddenly became still. This stillness turned into months escaping me. Much of this time was spent reflecting and analyzing some of the material I had gathered, however, nothing significant seemed to be coming my way. I had pages and pages of content, yet I decided to search for ideas beyond what I had already compiled. Search after search, I reached dead ends. Everything, along with this project, seemed inconclusive. During this delayed time, I experienced many personal life-changing moments myself.

To name one, I was unexpectedly laid off from my job. This was an extremely low and confusing point in my life. To simply put it, I felt like I had failed a million times. But instead of continuing to feed off of my internal panic, I kicked my heels to the side and decided to experience the world barefoot for a while. During my time off, I completed and presented my graduate thesis, I traveled, I landed a book contract with Skyhorse Publishing, who believed in my idea, graduated from graduate school, and within that six-month hiatus, landed an incredible career opportunity. Shortly after, my husband also gained the opportunity of a lifetime. We purchased our first home and moved. During my own personal journey to find happiness, purpose, and wisdom in every situation I encountered, I became effortlessly enlightened at the value of the simple things in life.

When I think about what I learned along the way, I am reminded of one older gentleman telling me that the best days of his life were during the Great Depression. Similarly, another individual who told me she admired and looked up to her friend who grew up in poverty, revealed that people can be fulfilled with very little.

What I have learned about wisdom is nearly transferrable but when I reflect on the responses I received, I am reminded that everything is within reach.

At first thought, wisdom appears as a topic that is mysterious and hard to achieve. I was wrong.

When I think of wisdom now, I think of things that are simple and natural. When I think of wisdom, I think of being with family, spending more time appreciating them, and creating more memories before it is too late. When I think of wisdom, I think of being in love, loving others, enhancing my relationships, and fulfilling my role as a friend, wife, and daughter. When I think of wisdom, I think of making the decision to live a happy, positive, and meaningful life. When I think of wisdom, I think of all matters close to the heart.

Wisdom, to me, is the ability to reflect on life and fully appreciate what is there. It does not need to take a lifetime to acquire wisdom and you don't need to look far.

Acknowledgments

To every single individual who contributed words of wisdom, thank you for sharing your empowering thoughts to inspire the lives of others. You are the reason this book is in our hands.

To those who have not yet contributed, allow this to be your platform. Help keep the wise words coming by sending your submissions to contact@thebookofwisdom.org or visit thebookofwisdom.org.